孔子学院总部／
国家汉办汉语国际推广成都基地规划教材

走进天府系列教材【成都印象】

饮川酒

Let's Drink Sichuan Liquor

西 南 财 经 大 学
汉语国际推广成都基地　　著

西南财经大学出版社
中国·成都

西 南 财 经 大 学
汉语国际推广成都基地 著

总策划 涂文涛

策 划
李永强

主 编
梁 婷 白巧燕

编 者
《成都印象·游成都》 胡倩琳
《成都印象·居成都》 郑 莹
《成都印象·吃川菜》 谢 娟 王 新
《成都印象·品川茶》 肖 静
《成都印象·饮川酒》 谢 娟
《成都印象·看川剧》 郑 莹
《成都印象·绣蜀绣》 谢 娟
《成都印象·梦三国之蜀国》 蒋林益 胡佩迦
《成都印象·悟道教》 沙 莎 吕 彦 陈 茉
《成都印象·练武术》 邓 帆 刘 亚

审 订 冯卫东

英文翻译
Alexander Demmelhuber

Introduction

Let's Drink Sichuan Liquor is one part of the "Impressions of Chengdu" textbook series, which is promoted by the Chengdu Base of Confucius Institute Headquarters and published by the Southwestern University of Finance and Economics. This book contains 8 units, which are designed on the basis of the Confucius Institute Headquarters' /Hanban's "International Curriculum for Chinese Language Education"(hereinafter referred to as "Curriculum"), as can be seen, for example, on vocabulary and language points used, and ensures that this textbook is held to scientific, systematic and rigorous standards.

Most of China's well-known brands of Luzhou-flavor liquor come from Sichuan because Sichuan's water, climate and pit mud lend themselves well for brewing. In 2007, Sichuan's liquor production of 860,000 tonnes surpassed Shandong Province's, making Sichuan the number one producer in China. By the end of 2016, Sichuan was still the nation's leading producer of liquor. This book starts with the classification and brewing methods of Sichuan liquor and gives an overview of the "six golden flowers" in Sichuan's liquor industry as well as of various drinking customs and anecdotes.

This book's vocabulary follows the "Outline Vocabulary of the New HSK" and the lessons contained herein are designed for readers at the HSK 4 level or above. For ease of understanding, the units are presented in narrative and dialog forms. We hope that this book lets our students experience the close relationship between liquor and life while they learn more about the basics of Sichuan liquor. At the same time, the book will hopefully broaden the cultural horizons of intermediate students of Chinese and comprehensively improve their language proficiency.

Hopefully, you will enjoy *Let's Drink Sichuan Liquor* and we are looking forward to any criticism or suggestions you might have. Hanban gave us much help and support during editing of this book and we would like to take this opportunity to express our gratitude.

Please note that 酒 is an umbrella term just like "alcoholic beverage"; however, the English is rather cumbersome and in many translations, "wine" or "liquor" is used as a catch-all term instead, regardless of accuracy. The translation of this book keeps with this convention.In East Asian countries, manufacture of alcoholic beverages is different than that found in Western countries. Rice wine, for example, is technically not a wine; its manufacturing method is more akin to beer brewing.

前　言

　　中国浓香型白酒的知名品牌大多来自四川，因为四川的水、气候和窖泥都特别适合酿酒。2007年，四川白酒以86万吨的产量超过山东省，成为中国第一。直到2016年年底，川酒产量仍然是全国第一。

　　《饮川酒》是西南财经大学汉语国际推广成都基地推出的《成都印象》系列教材之一。全书共8课，以孔子学院总部／国家汉办的《国际汉语教学通用课程大纲》为基本编写依据，涉及大纲中的大量词汇、语言点等指标，以保证教材的科学性、系统性和严谨性。本书从川酒的分类和川酒的酿造方面入手，介绍了川酒的"六朵金花"以及各种饮酒习俗和奇闻逸事，所使用词汇参照《新汉语水平考试词汇大纲》编排设计，适宜具有HSK4级以上水平的读者阅读。为了便于理解，全书以叙述和对话两种表现形式呈现。希望能让留学生在了解川酒基本知识的同时感受到酒与生活的紧密关系，同时希望能够扩宽初级汉语水平学生的文化视野，全面提升汉语水平。

　　希望您能喜欢我们的《饮川酒》这本教材，也希望您对本书提出批评和建议。本书的编写得到了国家汉办的大力支持和帮助，在此一并表示感谢。

目录

第一课 【酒仙李白】
Lesson 1 【Li Bai: Immortal of Wine】

① 李 白　Lǐ Bái
② 将进酒　Qiāng Jìn Jiǔ
③ 仙　xiān
④ 诗　shī
⑤ 代表作　dàibiǎozuò
⑥ 后 人　hòurén

王乐乐：
一华，你在房间做什么呢？

江一华：
乐乐，请进。我在看书。

王乐乐：
李白写的《将进酒》？看得懂吗？

江一华：
不太懂。你能介绍一下李白吗？

王乐乐：
李白是诗仙，也是酒仙。

江一华：
诗仙？

王乐乐：
他写了非常多的诗，他的很多诗都成了代表作，被后人学习。

⑦浪 漫　làngmàn
⑧怪不得　guàibude
⑨酒 量　jiǔliàng
⑩醉　zuì
⑪酒 度　jiǔdù

江一华：

他写了很多好的诗歌，所以叫诗仙。你说他也是酒仙，难道是因为他能喝很多酒吗？

王乐乐：

是的。李白爱喝酒，他喝了酒以后写出来的诗歌非常浪漫，非常美，而且，他的许多诗里也写到了酒。

江一华：

怪不得书里说李白一天要喝三百杯酒。他的酒量太大了！

王乐乐：

其实李白的酒量也不一定那么大。

江一华：

喝三百杯还不多吗？

王乐乐：

因为酒不一样。如果是现在的白酒，李白早就醉死了。李白那个时候喝的酒酒度很低，大概和现在的啤酒差不多，而且杯子也是非常小的杯子。

江一华：
    如果是这样的话，我应该也可以用他的杯子喝三百杯。

Wang Lele: Yihua, what are you doing in your room?

Jiang Yihua: Lele, come in. I'm reading.

Wang Lele: Li Bai's *Bring In the Wine*? Can you understand it?

Jiang Yihua: Not really. Can you tell me who he is?

Wang Lele: Li Bai was both an immortal of poetry and of wine.

Jiang Yihua: An immortal of poetry?

Wang Lele: He wrote a lot of poetry. Many of his poems became representative works and have been subjects of study for later generations.

Jiang Yihua: He wrote a lot of good poetry, which is why he is called an immortal of poetry. You said that he is also called an immortal of wine. Is it because he could drink a lot of alcohol?

Wang Lele: Correct. Li Bai loved drinking. The poems he wrote after drinking were very romantic and beautiful. Liquor is also the subject of many poems he wrote.

Jiang Yihua: No wonder the book says that Li Bai would drink three hundred cups of liquor a day. He could hold an enormous amount of liquor!

Wang Lele: Actually,he was not necessarily a good drinker.

Jiang Yihua: Drinking three hundred cups doesn't qualify as good?

Wang Lele: Because liquor was different back then. If he had had today's liquor, Li Bai would have quickly drunk himself to death. Back in his days, the alcohol content of liquor was low, about the same as today's beer, and the cups were also tiny.

Jiang Yihua: If that's the chase, I should also be able to drink 300 cups of liquor with his cup.

词语

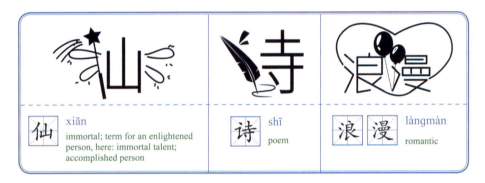

仙	xiān immortal; term for an enlightened person, here: immortal talent; accomplished person	诗	shī poem	浪 漫	làngmàn romantic

dài biǎo zuò 代 表 作	masterwork; representative work; magnum opus	hòu rén 后 人	later generations
guài bu de 怪 不 得	no wonder; no surprise	jiǔ liàng 酒 量	capacity for liquor (how much one can drink)
zuì 醉	drunk; intoxicated	jiǔ dù 酒 度	alcohol content

专有名词

1. 李白   / Lǐ Bái / Li Bai

2. 将进酒   / Qiāng Jìn Jiǔ / Bring In the Wine

语法点

1. 看得懂　　　　　　　　2. 难道是……吗？

思考

1. 你知道李白吗？请简单介绍一下李白。

2. 李白被称为"诗仙"，他写了很多好的诗歌，除了《将进酒》，你还学过他的什么诗歌？请介绍一下。

第二课 【酒的分类】
Lesson 2 【Liquor Classification】

中国是农业大国，经济的发展以农业为主，先进的农业技术带来了很多粮食。这些吃不完的粮食就被中国人做成了各种酒。中国是世界上最早做酒的国家之一。不同的材料，用不同的方法，就能做出不同的酒。

白酒又叫老白干，是中国特有的一种蒸馏酒。它是用酒曲发酵、蒸馏后得到的酒，酒度比较高，一般是 28°～68°。

啤酒是最古老的酒精饮料。啤酒是用大麦芽为主要材料做的。酒度比较低，一般为 2°～5°。

果酒是人类最早学会做的酒，它是用水果和酵母做的酒，酒里有很浓的水果味儿。很多水果都可以做酒，比如梅子、猕猴桃、橙等。果酒的酒度不高，一般为 8.5°～16.2°。

①	农业	nóngyè
②	先进	xiānjìn
③	粮食	liángshi
④	蒸馏	zhēngliú
⑤	酒曲	jiǔqū
⑥	发酵	fājiào
⑦	大麦芽	dàmàiyá
⑧	酵母	jiàomǔ
⑨	梅子	méizi
⑩	浓	nóng
⑪	营养	yíngyǎng
⑫	丰富	fēngfù
⑬	醪糟	láozāo
⑭	浸泡	jìnpào
⑮	蒸	zhēng
⑯	煮	zhǔ
⑰	猕猴桃	míhóutáo
⑱	橙	chéng

黄酒是很古老的一种酒，而且也是中国特有的。它是用谷物做的，酒度一般低于 20°。黄酒营养非常丰富，所以也叫作"液体蛋糕"。

米酒，又名醪糟，把江米浸泡、蒸煮然后加酒曲，放在 20 多摄氏度的环境里，30 小时左右就可

⑲ 效 果	xiàoguǒ	
⑳ 环 境	huánjìng	
㉑ 谷 物	gǔwù	
㉒ 龟寿酒	Guī Shòu Jiǔ	

以了。因为是用江米做的,所以也叫"江米酒"。米酒味道比较甜,酒度一般为 1° ～ 2°,受到很多人的欢迎。李白一天要喝三百杯酒,喝的就是这样的"酒"。

把一些中药放在 50° ～ 60° 的白酒里浸泡一段时间后得到的酒就是"药酒"。药和酒泡在一起可以提高药的效果。龟寿酒、劲酒就是药酒。

China is a large country of agriculture, with agriculture being the main economic driver. Advanced agricultural technology has brought a lot of grains. Leftover grain has been turned by the Chinese into all kinds of liquor. China is one of the earliest countries in the world to make alcohol. Different materials and different methods may yield different beverages.

Baijiu, or Laobaigan, is a type of distilled liquor special to China. It is fermented with jiuqu and the alcohol content after distillation is relatively high, usually from 28 to 68 percent.

Beer is the oldest alcoholic beverage. Beer is made of barley sprouts as the main material. Alcohol content is relatively low, usually between 2 and 5 percent.

Wine is the earliest alcoholic drink people learnt to make and is made with fruits and yeast. It has a rich, fruity taste. A lot of fruits can be made into wine, for example plums, kiwis, oranges and so on. Alcohol content is not high, generally between 8.5 to 16.2 percent.

Huangjiu is a very old type of wine and also unique to China. It is made of cereals and its alcohol content is generally below 20 percent. Huangjiu is extremely rich in nutrients and is therefore also called "liquid cake".

Rice wine, or fermented glutinous rice wine, is made by soaking, cooking and steaming polished glutinous rice and adding jiuqu. Then it is placed in an environment of about 20 degrees Celsius where it sits for approximately 30 hours. Since it is made of polished glutinous rice, the beverage is also called fermented glutinous rice wine. Its taste is rather sweet, and its alcohol content is generally between 1 and 2 percent, which makes it a very popular drink. It is this kind of wine that Li Bai would drink three hundred cups of a day.

Soak some traditional Chinese medicinal herbs in baijiu with 50 to 60 percent alcohol and you get "medicinal liquor". Soaking herbs in alcohol can improve their efficacy. Guishou Jiu and Jin Jiu are both medicinal liquor.

词语

农业　nóngyè　agriculture

环境　huánjìng　environment

蒸　zhēng　steam

xiān jìn 先 进	advanced	
zhēng liú 蒸 馏	distil	
fā jiào 发 酵	ferment	
jiào mǔ 酵 母	yeast	
yíng yǎng 营 养	nutrition; nourishment	

liáng shi 粮 食	grain
jiǔ qū 酒 曲	jiuqu; distiller's yeast
dà mài yá 大 麦 芽	barley sprout
nóng 浓	concentrated; dense; strong
fēng fù 丰 富	rich; abundant; plentiful

láo zāo 醪 糟	fermented glutinous rice wine	jìn pào 浸 泡	soak; immerse
zhǔ 煮	boil; cook	xiào guǒ 效 果	result; effect

专有名词

1. 龟寿酒 / Guīshòu Jiǔ / Guishou Jiu

2. 劲酒 / Jìn Jiǔ / Jin Jiu

语法点

1. v.+ 成   2. 把……v.在

思考

1. 文中提到的六种酒，它们的原料和制作方法有什么不同？

2. 你对哪种酒最感兴趣？

3. 你试过中国的药酒吗？觉得怎么样？

4. 在你们国家有些什么种类的酒？

第三课 【酒的制作】
Lesson 3 【Liquor Production】

① 厂　　　chǎng
② 制 作　　zhìzuò
③ 过 程　　guòchéng
④ 成 熟　　chéngshú
⑤ 晾　　　liàng
⑥ 过 滤　　guòlǜ

王乐乐：
　　一华, 你喝酒吗？

江一华：
　　我常常喝啤酒, 有时候喝点儿葡萄酒。

王乐乐：
　　那你知道它们是怎么做的吗？

江一华：
　　我知道。在美国的时候, 我去参观过一个葡萄酒厂, 我看过他们制作葡萄酒的过程。

王乐乐：
　　快给我们介绍介绍。

江一华：
　　简单地说就是他们把成熟的葡萄洗干净、晾干、发酵, 然后过滤。不过葡萄酒也有很多种, 有不同的制作方法。

⑦酿　造　niàngzào
⑧配　制　pèizhì

王乐乐：

　　说得太好了。葡萄酒的这种制作方法叫"酿造"，中国也有一些酒是这样做出来的。

江一华：

　　除了酿造以外，还有哪些制作方法呢？

王乐乐：

　　中国的酒的制作方法有酿造、蒸馏和配制三种。

⑨压　榨　　　yāzhà
⑩原汁原味　　yuánzhī yuánwèi
⑪代　表　　　dàibiǎo
⑫中草药　　　zhōngcǎoyào
⑬香　料　　　xiāngliào
⑭植　物　　　zhíwù
⑮保　健　　　bǎojiàn
⑯治　　　　　zhì
⑰提　取　　　tíqǔ
⑱剑南春　　　Jiàn Nán Chūn
⑲五粮液　　　Wǔ Liáng Yè
⑳药物学　　　yàowùxué
㉑兰　茂　　　LánMào
㉒《滇南本草》《Diān Nán Běn Cǎo》
㉓竹叶青　　　Zhú Yè Qīng
㉔人参酒　　　rénshēnjiǔ

　　酿造酒是把谷物、水果发酵，然后用提取或压榨的方法得到的酒。比如黄酒、果酒和啤酒就是酿造酒，它们的酒度一般低于20°。这些酒的最大特点就是原汁原味，营养丰富，适量饮用对身体有很大的好处。

　　酿造酒的酒度比较低，为了得到更高酒度的酒，人们想到了新的办法——蒸馏。把酒度低的酒经过很多次蒸馏，就能得到酒度比较高的蒸馏酒了，这就是我们常常说的白酒。一般来说，蒸馏酒的酒度高于60°。川酒里的剑南春、五粮液就是蒸馏酒的代表。

　　中国的配制酒是在白酒里加入中草药、香料、动物或植物等，经过浸泡、蒸煮等方法得到的酒。这些酒有的有保健作用，有的还可以治病。

　　明朝药物学家兰茂写了一本《滇南本草》，里面就介绍了很多做配制酒的方法。我们现在喝的配制酒以保健酒为主，比如竹叶青、人参酒等。

Wang Lele: Yihua, do you drink?

Jiang Yihua: I often drink beer, and sometimes some wine.

Wang Lele: Then do you know how they are made?

Jiang Yihua: I do. In the United States, I visited a winery and saw the process of making wine.

Wang Lele: Tell us more about it, would you?

Jiang Yihua: Put simply, they washed the ripe grapes, dried them in the air, let them ferment and then filtered them.

There are lots of different wines, though, with different ways of manufacturing.

Wang Lele: Well put! This method of making wine is called vinification and some alcoholic beverages are also made this way in China.

Jiang Yihua: Apart from vinification, what other production methods are there?

Wang Lele: China's alcohol production uses three methods: vinification (fermentation or brewing), distillation and compounding.

Fermentation is the method of letting cereals or fruits ferment and then refining them or extracting their juices by pressure. This method is used for making huangjiu, wine and beer; beverages with alcohol content of generally less than 20%. Their most prominent features are their natural tastes and flavors, high nutrition, and great health benefits when consumed in moderation.

The alcohol content of beverages made by fermentation leaves much to be desired. To manufacture drinks with higher alcohol content, people thought of a new way: distillation. By distilling drinks with low alcohol content many times, the result is distilled liquor with relatively high alcohol content, and nets us the commonly known Chinese spirit baijiu. In general, the alcohol content of distilled spirits is above 60%. Jiannanchu and Wuliangye are the signature spirits among Sichuan's alcoholic drinks.

China's compounded liquors are made by adding Chinese medicinal herbs, spices, animals and plants to baijiu, which are then soaked, steamed or boiled. Some of these spirits have health benefits; others may also have curative properties.

Ming Dynasty pharmacologist Lan Mao wrote the *Southern Yunnan Materia Medica* where he introduced a lot of compounding methods. Nowadays, the Chinese drink compounded spirits mainly for health benefits, such as Bamboo Leaf Green, Ginseng and many more liquors.

词 语

提 取	tíqǔ
	refine

植 物	zhíwù
	plant

晾	liàng
	dry by airing

chǎng 厂	factory; mill; plant; works
guò chéng 过 程	process
guò lù 过 滤	filter; filtrate
pèi zhì 配 制	compound
yuán zhī yuán wèi 原 汁 原 味	natural/original juice and taste; authentic; genuine
zhōng cǎo yào 中 草 药	Chinese herbal medicine; Chinese medicinal herbs

zhì zuò 制 作	make; manufacture
chéng shú 成 熟	mature
niàng zào 酿 造	make (wine, vinegar, soybean paste etc.) by fermentation; brew (beer, etc.); vinification
yā zhà 压 榨	extract (juice etc.) by pressure; press; squeeze
dài biǎo 代 表	representative
xiāng liào 香 料	spice; flavoring; condiment

bǎo jiàn 保 健	health care; health protection

zhì 治	cure; treat (a disease)

专 有 名 词

1. 剑南春   / Jiàn Nán Chūn / Jiannanchun
2. 五粮液   / Wǔ Liáng Yè / Wuliangye
3. 滇南本草   / Diān Nán Běn Cǎo / Southern Yunnan Materia Medica
4. 兰 茂   / Lán Mào / Lan Mao
5. 竹叶青   / Zhú Yè Qīng / Bamboo Leaf Green Liquor

语 言 点

1. 过
2. 除了……以外，还……
3. 对……有好处
4. 有的……有的……

将进酒

[唐]李白

君不见，黄河之水天上来，奔流到海不复回。

君不见，高堂明镜悲白发，朝如青丝暮成雪。

人生得意须尽欢，莫使金樽空对月。

天生我材必有用，千金散尽还复来。

烹羊宰牛且为乐，会须一饮三百杯。

岑夫子，丹丘生，将进酒，杯莫停。

与君歌一曲，请君为我倾耳听。

钟鼓馔玉不足贵，但愿长醉不复醒。

古来圣贤皆寂寞，惟有饮者留其名。

陈王昔时宴平乐，斗酒十千恣欢谑。

主人何为言少钱，径须沽取对君酌。

五花马，千金裘，呼儿将出换美酒，

与尔同销万古愁。

咏绿荔枝与荔枝绿

[北宋]黄庭坚

王公权家荔枝绿，廖致平家绿荔枝。

试倾一杯重碧色，快剥千颗轻红肌。

泼醅葡萄未足数，堆盘马乳不同时。

谁能品此胜绝味，惟有老杜东楼诗。

第四课 【川酒"六朵金花"】
Lesson 4 【"Six Golden Flowers" of Sichuan Liquor】

江一华：
　　喝了这么多种酒，我最喜欢的还是啤酒。

大萌：
　　我喜欢果酒。乐乐，你呢？

王乐乐：
　　我没特别喜欢的酒，不过我知道很多人喜欢白酒。

江一华：
　　是吗，四川最有名的白酒是什么？

大萌：
　　六朵金花。

江一华：
　　六朵金花？这是酒的名字？

⑥泸州老窖　Lúzhōu Lǎojiào
⑦沱牌曲酒　Tuópái Qūjiǔ
⑧全兴大曲　Quánxìng Dàqū
⑨郎　酒　　Láng Jiǔ

王乐乐：

这不是酒的名字。这是四川的六种白酒，它们在中国第五届评酒会上获得"国家名酒"称号，我们叫这六种酒"六朵金花"，它们分别是五粮液、泸州老窖、剑南春、沱牌曲酒、全兴大曲、郎酒。

江一华：

这六种酒有什么不一样吗？

王乐乐：

它们是用不同的粮食酿造的，酿造的方法不一样，酒度也不一样。

大萌：

它们的价格也不一样。

王乐乐：

是的，便宜的只要几百元，贵的要几千元。

⑩ 产 地　chǎndì
⑪ 连　　lián
⑫ 正 好　zhènghǎo

大萌：

我还知道一件有意思的事儿。

江一华：

什么事儿？快说说。

大萌：

六朵金花的产地也不一样。如果在地图上把它们的产地连在一起，正好是一个酒瓶的样子。

江一华：

太有意思了。六朵金花里哪种酒最好呢？

王乐乐：

应该是五粮液和剑南春吧。

（一）五粮液

五粮液是宜宾产的酒。这种酒已经有六百多年的历史了，但是最早的时候不叫这个名字。1909 年，在宜宾的一个聚会上，来了很多有名的人。吃饭的

①	主 人	zhǔrén
②	高 粱	gāoliang
③	糯 米	nuòmǐ
④	玉 米	yùmǐ
⑤	小 麦	xiǎomài
⑥	客 人	kèrén
⑦	改	gǎi
⑧	高 档	gāodàng

时候，主人拿出一瓶酒，大家都觉得非常香，都想知道酒的名字。主人介绍说："这种酒是用高粱、大米、糯米、玉米、小麦五种粮食做的，所以叫杂粮酒。"有一个客人说："这么香的酒，应该有一个更好听的名字。既然是用五种粮食做的，那么就叫五粮液吧。"大家都觉得新名字很好听。到1929年，这种酒就正式改名叫"五粮液"了。

现在的五粮液是中国最高档的白酒之一，价格也比较贵。但是五粮液酒厂新出的五粮春、金六福等酒的价格很便宜，味道也很好。

①	淡	dàn
②	称 赞	chēngzàn
③	三日开瓮香满域	
	sān rì kāi wèng xiāng mǎn yù	
④	玫 瑰	méiguī
⑤	到 底	dàodǐ
⑥	宜 宾	Yíbīn
⑦	五粮春	Wǔ Liáng Chūn
⑧	金六福	Jīn Liù Fú
⑨	绵 竹	Miánzhú
⑩	剑 山	Jiànshān

（二）剑南春

剑南春是四川绵竹的酒，最早出现在唐朝。那时，人们喜欢用"春"来做酒名，而绵竹在剑山南面，所以这酒就叫作"剑南春"。剑南春也是用高粱、大米、糯米、玉米、小麦五种谷物酿造的，有62°和52°两种酒度。不过剑南春的味道比五粮液淡一点儿，价格也便宜一些。

古时有人称赞这酒"三日开瓮香满域"。因为它像玫瑰一样香，所以也有人叫它"玫瑰老酒"。据说李白把身上穿的衣服卖了换钱，去买剑南春喝——那么剑南春到底有多好喝呢？

Jiang Yihua: After having had so many kinds of booze, I still like beer the most.

Da Meng: I like wine. Lele, what about you?

Wang Lele: I don't have any favorites, but I know a lot of people like drinking baijiu.

Jiang Yihua: Is that so? Does Sichuan have famous baijiu brands?

Da Meng: The six golden flowers.

Jiang Yihua: The six golden flowers? Is that the name of the drink?

Wang Lele: It's not. They are Sichuan's six kinds of baijiu and won the title of "China's Famous Spirits" at the Fifth China Wine & Spirits Awards. What is known as "the six golden flowers" are Wuliangye, Luzhou Laojiao, Jiannanchun, Tuopai Qu Liquor, Quanxing Daqu and Langjiu, respectively.

Jiang Yihua: What is the difference between these six spirits?

Wang Lele: They are made with different grains, their methods of manufacture are not the same and their alcohol contents also differ.

Da Meng: They're also priced differently.

Wang Lele: Right. From only a few hundred yuan for the cheapest to a few thousand yuan for the most expensive.

Da Meng: There's also an interesting little tidbit I know of.

Jiang Yihua: And what would that be? Tell us!

Da Meng: The six golden flowers are produced in different locations. If you connect the places on a map, they happen to form a liquor bottle.

Jiang Yihua: That is indeed interesting! What are the best liquors among the golden six flowers?

Wang Lele: I'd say Wuliangye and Jiannanchun.

[Part 1] Wuliangye

Wuliangye is a spirit from Yibin and has a history of more than 600 years. In the beginning, it was known by a different name. At a party in Yibin in 1909, a lot of famous people got together. During eating, the host presented a bottle of liquor. Everybody thought the drink tasted great and was eager to know its name. The host said, "This liquor is made of five grains, namely sorghum, rice, glutinous rice, corn and wheat, so its name is multi-grain spirit (Zaliangjiu)." One guest said, "Such a fragrant liquor, why don't give it a pretty name? Since it is made from five grains, what about five grain sap (Wuliangye)?" Everybody thought that was a great name. By 1929, this liquor was officially renamed "Wuliangye". Nowadays, Wuliangye is one of China's top-grade baijiu and is rather expensive. Having said that, Wuliangye Winery's new Wuliangchun, Jinliufu and other products are cheap and taste good.

[Part 2] Jiannanchun

Jiannanchun is a spirit from Mianzhu, Sichuan and made its earliest appearance in the Tang Dynasty. The people back then liked to use "chun" (spring) in the name of drinks, and since Mianzhu is located south of Jianshan, this spirit was named "Jiannanchun". Jiannanchun is also made of five grains, namely sorghum, rice, glutinous rice, corn and wheat, and is produced with two differing alcohol contents: 62% and 52%. Its taste, though, is a bit lighter than that of Wuliangye, and it is also a tad cheaper. In ancient times, some praised this spirit, saying "Opened after many a day in a jar, its fragrance fills the entire place". Since it is as fragrant as roses, the spirit is also called "rose liquor". It is said that Li Bai sold the very clothes on his body to buy some Jiannanchun – isn't that a testament to its taste?

26

词 语

小 麦 — xiǎomài — wheat

称 赞 — chēngzàn — praise

词	拼音	英文
届	jiè	measure word for meetings, congresses, etc.
获 得	huò dé	win
分 别	fēn bié	respectively
连	lián	link; join; connect
主 人	zhǔ rén	host
糯 米	nuò mǐ	glutinous rice
评 酒 会	píng jiǔ huì	wine & spirits competition
称 号	chēng hào	title
产 地	chǎn dì	place of production (or origin)
正 好	zhèng hǎo	happen to
高 粱	gāo liang	sorghum
客 人	kè rén	guest

gǎi 改	change; alter
dàn 淡	light (in taste)
sān rì kāi 三 日 开 wèng xiāng 瓮 香 mǎn yù 满 域	Opened after many a day in a jar, its fragrance fills the entire place.

gāo dàng 高 档	high grade; top grade; superior quality
méi guī 玫 瑰	rose
dào dǐ 到 底	in a question for emphasis
yù mǐ 玉 米	corn; maize

专 有 名 词

1. 宜 宾　/ Yíbīn/ Yibin

2. 五粮春　/ Wǔ Liáng Chūn / Wuliangchun

3. 金六福　/ Jīn liù Fú / Jinliufu

4. 绵 竹　/ Miánzhú / Mianzhu

5. 剑 山　/ Jiànshān / Jianshan

语言点

1. 既然……那么……

思考

1. 中国最好的三种白酒"茅五剑"，你知道是什么酒吗？

2. 川酒的六朵金花各自有什么特点？请简单介绍一下。

3. 川酒有了新的"六朵金花"，你知道是哪些吗？请查阅资料，然后跟同学们分享一下。

4. 在你们国家有些什么名酒？请简单介绍一下。

第五课 【饮酒习俗】
Lesson 5 【Drinking Customs】

① 神　　shén
② 祖 先　zǔxiān
③ 享 用　xiǎngyòng
④ 祭 祀　jìsì

江一华：
中国人为什么这么喜欢喝白酒呢？

王乐乐：
酒是用粮食酿造的，是很好的东西，在一些重要的时候我们要把酒给神和祖先享用。

江一华：
重要的时候是什么时候？

王乐乐：
比如祭祀的时候，比如战争前，都要喝酒。

江一华：
真有意思。

王乐乐：
还有中国的一些重要的节日，我们也喝酒。

大概从汉武帝时候开始，正月初一被定为春节。这一天中国人要喝屠苏酒，希望长寿。中国人也用酒来祭祀神和祖先，希望得到他们的保护，希望在新的一年里健康好运。阳历4月5日是清明节。人们去给祖先扫墓的时候，先要打扫坟墓周围，然后用美食和美酒来祭祀。农历五月初五是端午节，人们喝菖蒲酒和雄黄酒来驱虫防病。农历八月十五是中秋节，在这个家人团圆的节日里，我们喝着桂花酒赏月。九月初九重阳节要爬上高山喝菊花酒。一年最后一天叫除夕，这天晚上全家团圆，要喝团圆酒。

① 正　月　　zhēngyuè
② 阳　历　　yánglì
③ 长　寿　　chángshòu
④ 扫　墓　　sǎomù
⑤ 农　历　　nónglì
⑥ 驱虫防病　qūchóng fángbìng

① 礼仪之邦　lǐyí zhībāng
② 礼　　　　lǐ
③ 习　俗　　xísú
④ 平　时　　píngshí
⑤ 酒　德　　jiǔdé
⑥ 遵　守　　zūnshǒu

江一华：

中国是礼仪之邦，中国人的生活里有很多"礼"。那么喝酒的时候应该也有"礼"吧？

王乐乐：

当然。酒与礼从来都分不开。不同的节日人们有不同的喝酒习俗，而且平时喝酒也要注意酒德。

江一华：

真有意思。

王乐乐：

酒德就是喝酒的时候一定要遵守的"礼"。和酒德好的人喝酒，会让人觉得快乐。

中国人爱喝酒、会喝酒。喝酒的时候有很多"礼"，这就是"酒德"。酒德包括很多内容，最重要的有三个方面：

第一，敬酒。如果你是主人，那么在吃饭之前应该说敬酒辞，然后和大家干杯。一般来说，第一杯酒应该要喝完。如果你是客人，在主人敬酒以后，应该回敬主人。不管主人还是客人，都应该注意，敬酒的时候要站起来、微笑着、手拿酒杯、看着对方说话或者喝酒。如果没有什么特别的人，那么敬酒的时候就从左到右或者从右到左一个一个地敬酒。如果你真的不能喝酒，那么应该先跟大家说清楚，在喝酒的时候可以"以茶代酒"。

第二，喝酒的速度。喝酒的速度太快是不礼貌的。如果你是客人，那么尽量不要比主人快。特别是女子，要慢慢喝，不然别人会以为你是酒鬼。而且慢慢喝也不太容易喝醉。

第三，喝酒的量。汉语里说"君子饮酒，三杯为度"，意思是，要注意自己的酒量，不能喝太多，不能喝醉。

① 敬　　　jìng
② 辞　　　cí
③ 速　度　sùdù
④ 礼　貌　lǐmào
⑤ 尽　量　jǐnliàng
⑥ 不　然　bùrán
⑦ 君　子　jūnzǐ
⑧ 度　　　dù
⑨ 汉武帝　Hàn Wǔ Dì
⑩ 屠苏酒　Tú Sū Jiǔ
⑪ 菖　蒲　chāngpú
⑫ 雄　黄　xiónghuáng
⑬ 桂　花　guìhuā
⑭ 重阳节　Chóngyáng Jié
⑮ 菊　花　júhuā

Jiang Yihua: Why do the Chinese like drinking baijiu so much?

Wang Lele: It is made from grain and as such is good stuff. On important occasions, we also let gods and our ancestors enjoy drinks.

Jiang Yihua: When are these important occasions?

Wang Lele: The Chinese always drink when offering sacrifices to the gods or ancestors or before a war, for example.

Jiang Yihua: Fascinating!

Wang Lele: There are also some important Chinese holidays when we also drink.

Probably starting with Emperor Wu of the Han Dynasty, the first day of the first lunar month was designated as the Spring Festival. On this day, the Chinese drink tusu in hopes of a long life. They also use alcohol as a sacrifice in gods and ancestor worship, hoping that they will receive their protection and that they will be healthy and lucky in the new year. Tomb-Sweeping Day is on April 5 in the Gregorian calendar. When people go to their ancestors' graves for sweeping, they must first clean the area around the grave and then offer delicious food and alcoholic beverages as sacrifice. The fifth day of the fifth lunar month is the Dragon Boat Festival when people drink calamus and realgar wines to expel intestinal worms and prevent disease. August 15 in the lunar calendar is the Mid-autumn Festival. During this festival of family reunion, the Chinese drink osmanthus-scented alcohol while enjoying a beautiful full moon. On the Double Ninth Festival in early September, Chinese people climb mountains and drink chrysanthemum wine. The last day of the (lunar) year is (Lunar) New Year's Eve when the whole family come together and drink reunion wine.

Jiang Yihua: China is a land of ceremony and propriety. "Ceremonies" are an important part of life in China. So, I suppose there are also ceremonies during drinking?

Wang Lele: Of course. Alcohol and ceremony are inseparable. People have different drinking customs for different festivals, and also adhere to certain drinking manners when having alcohol.

Jiang Yihua: What are drinking manners?

Wang Lele: During drinking, you have to comply with the "ceremony". Drinking alcohol will well-mannered people will make everyone happy.

The Chinese love and are very particular about drinking. When they drink, there are a lot of "ceremonies", or "drinking manners", to adhere to. The three most important aspects are:

1)Toasting. If you are the host, you ought to say some words and propose a toast before eating. In general, the first cup of alcohol should be emptied all at once. If you are a guest, you should propose a toast back to the host after the host propose theirs. Whether you are the host or the guest, you should keep in mind to stand up, smile, hold a cup with alcohol and look at the others when toasting. If there are no special people present, then toasting starts from left to right or right to left one by one. If you cannot drink alcohol at all, then make that first clear to everyone and drink tea instead.

2)The speed of drinking. Drinking too fast is impolite. If you are a guest, try not to be faster than the host, particularly if you are a woman: drink slowly, otherwise the others will think that you are an alcoholic. Furthermore, if you drink slowly, you will not get drunk as easily.

3)The amount of drinking. There is a saying in China: "A gentleman only drinks three cups of wine", which means that you must pay attention to how much you drink. You should not drink too much and get drunk.

词 语

| 君 子 | jūnzǐ (originally a Confucian term, meaning an ideal man whose character embodies the virtue of benevolence, and who acts in accordance with the rites and rightness) gentleman; nobleman; person of noble character | 速 度 | sùdù speed; rate; pace; tempo |

shén 神	god; deity	zǔ xiān 祖 先	ancestors; ancestry; forebears; forefathers
xiǎng yòng 享 用	enjoy (the use of)	jì sì 祭 祀	offer sacrifices (to gods or ancestors)
zhēng yuè 正 月	first month of the lunar year; first moon	yáng lì 阳 历	solar calendar; Gregorian calendar
cháng shòu 长 寿	long life; longevity	sǎo mù 扫 墓	sweep the grave or tomb (of one's ancestors) (pay respects to a dead person at his grave or tomb)
nóng lì 农 历	the traditional Chinese calendar; the lunar calendar	qū chóng fáng bìng 驱 虫 防 病	expel intestinal worms and prevent disease (drinking realgar is believed to detoxify the body)
lǐ yí zhī bāng 礼仪之邦	glutinous riceland of ceremony and propriety	lǐ 礼	ceremony; rite; ritual; courtesy; etiquette; manners

xí sú 习 俗	custom; convention; usual practice		píng shí 平 时	ordinarily; generally
jiǔ dé 酒 德	propriety in drinking; drinking manners; drinking etiquette		zūn shǒu 遵 守	observe; abide by; comply with; follow
jìng 敬	salute; offer; honor; show respect to		dù 度	limit
bù rán 不 然	or else; otherwise		cí 辞	word; statement; speech
lǐ mào 礼 貌	courtesy; politeness; manners		jǐn liàng 尽 量	as much as possible; to the greatest extent
jiǔ guǐ 酒 鬼	drunkard; wine bibber; toper; alcoholic			

专 有 名 词

1. 汉武帝 / Hàn Wǔ Dì / Emperor Wu of the Han Dynasty

2. 屠苏酒 / Tú Sū Jiǔ / tusu

3. 重阳节 / Chóng Yáng Jié / Double Ninth Festival; Chung Yeung Festival

语言点

1. V.+ 着……　　　2. 如果……，那么……

3. 以……代……

思考

1. 你和中国人喝过酒吗？他们喝酒的时候都有些什么习俗、习惯？

2. 中国有酒文化，喝酒的时候讲究酒德，如果你失了酒德，会让大家都不愉快。除了文中提到的三种酒德，你还知道一些什么酒德？

3. 在你们国家，喝酒有些什么习俗？

第六课 【酒与健康】
Lesson 6 【Liquor and Health】

大萌：

　　果酒和白酒相比，我更喜欢白酒。

江一华：

　　我对白酒也挺感兴趣的，我在看历史故事的
时候发现，很多故事都和酒有关系，故事里
的人都爱喝酒。

大萌：

　　是啊。节日要喝酒，聚会要喝酒，一个人吃
饭也可以自己喝酒；做菜可以放酒，做药也
可以放酒。白酒对中国人的影响太大了。

王乐乐：

　　因为适量喝点儿白酒对身体有好
处啊。

江一华：

　　有什么好处？

① 适量　shìliàng
② 提供　tígōng
③ 热量　rèliàng
④ 放松　fàngsōng
⑤ 兴奋　xīngfèn
⑥ 熟悉　shúxī

王乐乐：

很多啊。比如说白酒里有很多营养，也能给身体提供热量。在北方很冷的季节，人们常常会喝一点儿酒，喝了酒以后，就会觉得没那么冷了。而且适量喝酒能让我们放松，没那么累。对于常常睡得不好的人来说，睡觉前适量喝酒，还能帮助他睡得更好。

大萌：

聚会喝酒是因为酒让人们兴奋，喝了酒会变得更热情，这时候就算不熟悉的人，也能很快变成好朋友。

江一华：

虽然喝酒有这么多好处，但是白酒的酒度太高了，我还是觉得不太好。

王乐乐：

的确是这样。有些人常常忘记应该适量喝酒，他们喝高兴了，就随便喝，最后喝醉了，发生很多对自己、对别人、对社会都很不好的事儿。

Da Meng: Choosing between wine and baijiu, I'd go with baijiu.

Jiang Yihua: Baijiu has also stricken my fancy. When I was reading historical stories, I noticed that many of them are about alcohol and the people in those stories love drinking.

Da Meng: Absolutely! We drink on holidays and when we get together with others. If you eat by yourself, you can also have some alcohol. You can use it for cooking and for making medicine. Alcohol plays quite a big role in China.

Wang Lele: That's because moderate consumption of alcohol is good for your health.

Jiang Yihua: What are the health benefits?

Wang Lele: There are tons of them. For example, baijiu is very nutritious and provides your body with heat. During the colder months in the North, the people often drink a little bit of alcohol, so they don't feel too cold. Moderate drinking also helps us relax and be not as stressed out. For those who often don't sleep well, having some alcohol before going to bed helps them sleep better.

Da Meng: We drink during get-togethers because alcohol makes us excited and warms up the atmosphere. When that happens, even strangers turn quickly into friends.

Jiang Yihua: There are lots of benefits for drinking alcohol, but baijiu contains too much alcohol, I still don't think it's a great idea.

Wang Lele: This is indeed true. Some often forget that they should drink in moderation. When they're in high spirits, they simply chug it down and get drunk, which leads to many bad things happen to themselves, to others and to society.

词语

兴 奋	xīngfèn
	be excited

热 量	rèliàng
	heat; calorific value

shì liàng	
适 量	appropriate amount
fàng sōng	
放 松	relax; loosen

tí gōng	
提 供	furnish;supply; offer; provide
shú xī	
熟 悉	be familiar with; know well

语言点

1. 对于……来说   2. 就算……也……

思考

1. 你觉得喝酒的好处多还是坏处多？请举例说明。

2. 我们应不应该喝酒？应该怎么喝酒？

第七课 【名人与酒】
Lesson 7 【Legends About Famous Figures and Liquor】

江一华：

中国人这么爱喝酒，应该有很多跟酒有关系的故事吧？

王乐乐：

当然有。

大萌：

而且有很多。

王乐乐：

是的。有的人一生都离不开酒；有的人因为酒成了英雄；有的人因为酒失去了很多重要的东西；有的人的爱情跟酒有很大的关系；有的人因为酒交到了最好的朋友。

① 失去　　shīqù

①夸	kuā
②吹牛	chuīniú
③于是	yúshì
④记账	jìzhàng
⑤改天	gǎitiān
⑥浇	jiāo
⑦晋代	Jìn Dài
⑧杜康	Dù Kāng
⑨刘伶	Liú Líng

（一）杜康酿酒醉刘伶

　　传说在晋代，杜康是酒酿得最好的人，刘伶是当时酒量最大的人。杜康夸自己的酒是"不醉三年不要钱"，刘伶觉得杜康吹牛，所以进店开始喝酒。他喝了三杯就醉了，说"真是好酒！可是我忘了带钱，你先记账，改天我来还你"。刘伶回到家就睡着了，一睡就是三年，三年后杜康来刘伶家收酒钱，刘伶才醒过来。后来人们用"喝了杜康三杯酒，醉了刘伶三年整"来称赞杜康的酒。刘伶和杜康也因为这件事变成了很好的朋友。

①唐玄宗	Táng Xuánzōng
②杨贵妃	Yáng Guìfēi
③一口气	yīkǒuqì
④到处	dàochù
⑤漂泊	piāobó
⑥影子	yǐngzi
⑦掉	diào
⑧捞	lāo
⑨淹	yān

（二）李白生于酒了于酒

　　李白是唐朝很有名的诗人，他在四川长大。李白一生都离不开酒，他一共写了1 500多首诗，其中跟酒有关系的诗就有200多首。

　　传说有一次，唐玄宗让李白为杨贵妃写诗，可是李白喝醉了。唐玄宗没办法，就叫人用冷水把李白浇醒。醒来后的李白一口气写出了十几篇很美的诗。

　　晚年的李白到处漂泊，日子过得很苦。有一天晚上他在船上喝酒，喝醉了，看到水里月亮的影子，以为是真的月亮掉进水里了，于是伸手去捞，结果自己不小心掉进江里淹死了……不过这只是一个传说，是对李白的死的一种猜想而已。

⑩猜　想　cāixiǎng
⑪而　已　éryǐ

（三）武松醉打老虎

在小说《水浒传》里讲了很多英雄的故事，其中最精彩的就是武松打虎的故事。

一天，武松回家看哥哥。他经过一个叫景阳冈的地方，这儿有一种酒度非常高的酒，被大家称为"三碗不过冈"——喝了三碗酒一定会醉，不能走过景阳冈。武松不相信，他喝了三碗以后继续赶路，在景阳冈上开始觉得头晕——他喝醉了。这时候出现了一只大老虎。喝了酒的武松有点儿兴奋，也不觉得害怕，他借着酒劲，用拳头打死了老虎。后来人们知道了这件事，称赞武松是"打虎英雄"。

①英　雄　yīngxióng
②精　彩　jīngcǎi
③继　续　jìxù
④赶　　　gǎn
⑤晕　　　yūn
⑥害　怕　hàipà
⑦酒　劲　jiǔjìn
⑧水浒传　Shuǐhǔ Zhuàn
⑨武　松　Wǔ Sōng
⑩景阳冈　Jǐngyáng Gāng
⑪拳　头　quántóu

（四）文君卖酒

司马相如是西汉时有名的文人，卓文君是蜀中四大才女之一。他们俩一见钟情。不过那个时候的司马相如没有钱，所以卓文君的父亲不同意他们俩在一起。没有办法，他们俩只能偷偷到了成都。后来他们把贵的东西都卖了，买了一个酒铺。卓文君每天在酒铺卖酒。卓文君和司马相如为了能跟自己爱的人在一起，克服了所有的困难。慢慢地，大家都知道了他们的故事。后来，只要人们说到美好的爱情就会想到卓文君和司马相如的故事。

①文　人　wénrén
②一见钟情　yījiàn zhōngqíng
③偷　偷　tōutōu
④酒　铺　jiǔpù
⑤克　服　kèfú
⑥司马相如　Sīmǎ Xiàngrú
⑦西　汉　Xī Hàn
⑧卓文君　Zhuó Wénjūn
⑨蜀　　　Shǔ

Jiang Yihua: The Chinese love drinking, so there should be a lot of stories related to alcohol, right?

Wang Lele: There sure are.

Da Meng: And there are many.

Wang Lele: Yes. Some simply cannot do without alcohol; some turn into heroes because of alcohol; some lose a lot of important things due to drinking; some people's love is closely connected with booze; and others become best friends thanks to alcohol.

[Part 1] Du Kang Makes Liu Ling Drunk

This is a legend that took place in the Jin Dynasty. Du Kang was known as the best brewer, and Liu Ling as the best drinker. Du Kang bragged, "if my booze does not make you drunk for three years, you will get your money back". Liu Ling thought Du Kang was just talking big, so he went into Du Kang's store and began drinking. He became drunk after three cups and said, "It really is good stuff! I forgot to bring money, though, you first keep tab. I'll come back later and pay you." Liu Ling went home and promptly fell asleep. He slept for three years. After three years, when Du Kang went to Liu Ling's place to collect his money, Liu Ling woke up. Later on, people praised Du Kang's drinks by saying "having three cups of Du Kang's liquor makes Liu Ling drunk for three whole years". Liu Ling and Du Kang became good friends because of this incident.

[Part 2]Liu Bai: Born Drinking, Died Drinking

Li Bai was a famous Tang poet, who grew up in Sichuan. He couldn't do without wine his entire life. He wrote more than 1,500 poems in total, 200 of which are related to wine.

Legend has it that one day, Emperor Xuanzong of Tang wanted Li Bai to write poems for Lady Yang, but Li Bai was drunk. The emperor saw no other way than to have cold water poured on Li Bai, which woke him up. Li Bai then wrote a dozen beautiful poems in one go.

In old age, Li Bai was drifting about the land and he led a bitter life. One night, he was drinking on a boat and got drunk. He saw the reflection of the moon in the water and thought that the real moon fell into the water. He wanted to scoop it out. As he reached out, he accidentally fell into the river and drowned. Having said that, that is just a legend and merely a conjecture on Li Bai's death, nothing more.

[Part 3] Wu Song Drunkenly Slays a Tiger

The novel *Water Margin* tells a lot of heroic stories; one of the most exciting ones is the story of Wu Song Drunkenly Slaying a Tiger.

One day, Wu Song went home to see his brother. He was passing by a place called Jingyang Ridge, where he had liquor containing an extremely high amount of alcohol. It was said that "after three bowls, you are unable to pass the ridge", meaning that after three bowls of this liquor, you will definitely be drunk and will be unable to walk past Jingyang Ridge. Wu Song did not believe that. He drank three bowls and hastily continued his journey. On Jingyang Ridge, he began to feel dizzy – he was drunk. It was at this point that a big tiger appeared. Drunk as he was, Wu Song felt excited and was not scared. Exhilarated by the alcohol, he killed the tiger with his fist. Later, when others learned about this deed, Wu Song was praised as the "Tiger Slayer".

[Part 4] Wenjun Sells Wine

Sima Xiangru was a famous scholar during Western Han Dynasty; Zhuo Wenjun was one of the four most talented women in Sichuan. They both fell in love at first sight; however, at that time, Sima Xiangru had no money, so Zhuo Wenjun's father did not agree the two of them being together. They saw no other way but stealing themselves away to Chengdu. Then they sold every precious thing they had and bought a wine shop, where Wenjun sold wine every day. Zhuo Wenjun and Sima Xiangru overcame all difficulties in order to be together. Slowly, their story spread. Later, when people talked about happy love, they thought of Zhuo Wenjun and Sima Xiangru's story.

词语

影 子	yǐngzi
	shadow; reflection

拳 头	quántóu
	fist

shī qù 失 去	lose		kuā 夸	boast; exaggerate; praise
chuī niú 吹 牛	boast; brag; talk big		yú shì 于 是	as a result; thus; consequently
jì zhàng 记 账	keep accounts; keep tab; charge to an account		gǎi tiān 改 天	another day; some other time
jiāo 浇	pour (liquid on)		yī kǒu qì 一 口 气	in one breath; without a break; at one go
dào chù 到 处	everywhere		piāo bó 漂 泊	lead a wandering life; drift
diào 掉	fall; drop		lāo 捞	scoop out from a liquid; dredge up; fish up

yān 淹	drown
jīng cǎi 精 彩	wonderful; marvelous; brilliant
gǎn 赶	hurry
hài pà 害 怕	be afraid; be scared
wén rén 文 人	man of letters; scholar; literati
tōu tōu 偷 偷	stealthily; secretly; covertly; furtively; on the sly
kè fú 克 服	surmount; overcome

cāi xiǎng 猜 想	guess; conjecture
yīng xióng 英 雄	hero; heroic
jì xù 继 续	continue; go on
yūn 晕	dizzy
jiǔ jìn 酒 劲	alcoholic strength; strength gained through alcohol consumption
yī jiàn zhōng qíng 一 见 钟 情	fall in love at first sight
jiǔ pù 酒 铺	tavern; wine shop

专有名词

1. 晋代 / Jìn Dài /
the Jin Dynasty (265-420)

2. 杜康 / Dù Kāng / Du Kang

3. 刘伶 / Liú Líng / Liu Ling

4. 水浒传 / Shuǐhǔ Zhuàn /
Heroes of the Marshes or
Water Margin (a Chinese
novel of the early Ming
Dynasty by 施耐庵)

5. 唐玄宗 / Táng Xuánzōng / Emperor
Xuanzong of Tang (810-859)

6. 武松 / Wǔ Sōng / Wu Song

7. 景阳冈 / Jǐngyáng Gāng / Jingyang Ridge

8. 杨贵妃 / Yáng Guìfēi /
Lady Yang; Yang Guifei (719-756),
famous Tang beauty, consort of
Emperor Xuanzong

思考

1. 你还知道哪些中国的名人和酒的
故事？请讲给大家听。

2. 在你们国家有哪些名人爱喝酒？
他们有些什么有意思的故事？请讲
给大家听。

【 古诗里的川酒 】

Lesson 8　【 Sichuan Liquor in Ancient Poetry 】

①思如泉涌　sīrú quányǒng
②壮　　　　zhuàng
③胆　　　　dǎn
④勇 敢　　yǒnggǎn
⑤面 对　　miànduì
⑥现 实　　xiànshí
⑦敢　　　　gǎn
⑧敏 感　　mǐngǎn
⑨神 奇　　shénqí

江一华：

为什么很多文人都喜欢喝点儿酒呢？

大 萌：

他们高兴了喝酒，不高兴了也喝酒。

王乐乐：

是的。我想可能是因为酒能让他们兴奋起来，思如泉涌；或者可能是"酒能壮人胆"，能让他们更勇敢地面对现实，说出平时不敢说的话；也有可能是因为酒能让他们变得敏感，发现平时没有发现的情感。

江一华：

酒真的是很神奇的东西。

咏绿荔枝与荔枝绿

[北宋]黄庭坚

王公权家荔枝绿，廖致平家绿荔枝。
试倾一杯重碧色，快剥千颗轻红肌。
泼醅葡萄未足数，堆盘马乳不同时。
谁能品此胜绝味，惟有老杜东楼诗。

　　这首诗是黄庭坚在戎州（现在的宜宾市）的时候写的。王公权和廖致平都是黄庭坚的好朋友。有一次，他们三个人一起吃饭，廖致平带来了他家的绿荔枝，这种荔枝因为荔枝皮上红绿相间，很特别，所以叫"绿荔枝"。王公权家里是酿酒的，他带来了家里最好的"荔枝绿"酒。黄庭坚吃到了好吃的绿荔枝，喝到了好喝的"荔枝绿"酒。他把它们称赞为"戎州第一"。这个"荔枝绿"酒就是现在的"五粮液"。

① 荔枝　　lìzhī
② 皮　　　pí
③ 戎州　　Róngzhōu
④ 黄庭坚　Huáng Tíngjiān
⑤ 王公权　Wáng Gōngquán
⑥ 廖致平　Liào Zhìpíng

将进酒

[唐]李白

君不见，黄河之水天上来，奔流到海不复回。

君不见，高堂明镜悲白发，朝如青丝暮成雪。

人生得意须尽欢，莫使金樽空对月。

天生我材必有用，千金散尽还复来。

烹羊宰牛且为乐，会须一饮三百杯。

岑夫子，丹丘生，将进酒，杯莫停。

与君歌一曲，请君为我倾耳听。

钟鼓馔玉不足贵，但愿长醉不复醒。

古来圣贤皆寂寞，惟有饮者留其名。

陈王昔时宴平乐，斗酒十千恣欢谑。

主人何为言少钱，径须沽取对君酌。

五花马，千金裘，呼儿将出换美酒，与尔同销万古愁。

① 相 间　xiāngjiàn
② 古 代　gǔdài
③ 理 想　lǐxiǎng
④ 自 由　zìyóu
⑤ 现 实　xiànshí
⑥ 却　què
⑦ 权　quán
⑧ 解貂续酒　jiě diāo xù jiǔ

可以说，李白是中国古代诗人的代表，而这首诗是李白诗的代表。在李白的理想里，生活应该是浪漫的、自由的，可是现实的生活却很不一样。这让他很痛苦，可能他觉得钱和权都不重要，最重要的就是诗、酒和自由吧。所以他的诗离不开酒，离不开自由的想象。据说李白没钱买酒的时候还"解貂续酒"——把自己的衣服卖了换钱买酒喝，买的酒就是现在的"剑南春"酒。

Jiang Yihua: Why do so many scholars like drinking alcohol?

Da Meng: When they're happy, they'll drink; when they're unhappy, they'll drink as well.

Wang Lele: True. I think it's maybe because alcohol can make them feel excited and make ideas well up in their minds; or maybe it's because "alcohol can make them strong", allowing them to bravely face reality and say what they usually don't dare to say; maybe it's because alcohol can make them be sensitive and help them find emotions they usually don't feel.

Jiang Yihua: Alcohol really is amazing.

The poem on the top of page 55 is one Huang Tingjian wrote during his time in Rongzhou (now Yibin). Wang Gongquan and Liao Zhiping were both good friends with Huang Tingjian. One day, when the three of them were dining together, Liao Zhiping brought some green lychees from his home. They are called green lychees because their skin is red interspersed with green, making them look unique. Wang Gongquan's family is one of winemakers, so he also brought his family's best green lychee wine. Huang Tingjian ate the delicious green lychees and drank the tasty green lychee wine. He praised them as "Rongzhou's Finest". This green lychee wine is today's Wuliangye.

One could say that Li Bai was a representative of China's ancient poets, and this poem was his signature work. According to Li Bai, in a perfect world, life should be romantic and free, but real life is not like that at all. This pained him deeply because power and money probably were not important to him, but rather poems, liquor and freedom. This is why his poem is all about liquor, all about freedom. It is said that during the Tang Dynasty, when Li Bai had no money to buy alcohol, he rid himself of his furs to continue drinking, meaning he sold his clothes to have money for liquor. The drink he bought is today's Jiannanchun.

词语

壮	zhuàng strengthen; make better	
权	quán power	
古 代	gǔdài ancient times; (the period in Chinese history from remote antiquity down until the mid-19th century)	

sī rú quán yǒng 思 如 泉 涌	ideas teeming (or welling up) in one's mind
yǒng gǎn 勇 敢	brave; courageous
xiàn shí 现 实	reality
mǐn gǎn 敏 感	sensitive
lì zhī 荔 枝	litchi; lychee
xiāng jiàn 相 间	alternate with; intersperse with

dǎn 胆	courage; guts; bravery
miàn duì 面 对	face; confront
gǎn 敢	be brave enough; dare
shén qí 神 奇	magical; mystical; miraculous; amazing
pí 皮	skin
lǐ xiǎng 理 想	ideal; dream; perfect

zì yóu 自 由	freedom; liberty; unrestrained	què 却	but; yet; however
quán 权	power	jiě diāo xù jiǔ 解貂续酒	sell furs to continue drinking

专有名词

1. 戎州 / Róngzhōu / Rongzhou

2. 黄庭坚 / Huáng Tíngjiān / Huang Tingjian

3. 王公权 / Wáng Gōngquán / Wang Gongquan

4. 廖致平 / Liào Zhìpíng / Liao Zhiping

思考

1. 你还知道哪些中国跟酒有关的诗歌？请介绍给大家。

2. 在你们国家，文学作品和酒有关系吗？哪些文学作品和酒有关系？请举例说明。

参考文献
［References］

[1] 曾庆双. 中国白酒文化 [M]. 重庆：重庆大学出版社，2013.
[2] 范晓清. 酒与现代养生 [M]. 北京：人民军医出版社，2007.
[3] 郑宏峰. 中华酒典 [M]. 北京：线装书局，2008.

图书在版编目（CIP）数据

成都印象／西南财经大学 汉语国际推广成都基地著 —成都：西南财经
大学出版社，2019.7
（走进天府系列教材）
ISBN 987-7-5504-3776-0

Ⅰ.①成… Ⅱ.①西… Ⅲ.①汉语—对外汉语教学—教材②成都—
概况 Ⅳ.①H 195.4②K 927.11
中国版本图书馆 CIP 数据核字（2018）第 241717 号

走进天府系列教材：成都印象·饮川酒
ZOUJIN TIANFU XILIE JIAOCAI:CHENGDU YINXIANG·YIN CHUANJIU

西南财经大学　汉语国际推广成都基地　著

策　　划：王正好　何春梅
责任编辑：李　才
装帧设计：张艳洁
插　　画：辣点设计
责任印制：朱曼丽

出版发行	西南财经大学出版社（四川省成都市光华村街 55 号）
网　　址	http：//www.bookcj.com
电子邮件	bookcj@ foxmail.com
邮政编码	610074
电　　话	028-87353785
照　　排	上海辣点广告设计咨询有限公司
印　　刷	四川新财印务有限公司
成品尺寸	170mm×240mm
印　　张	46.5
字　　数	875 千字
版　　次	2019 年 7 月第 1 版
印　　次	2019 年 7 月第 1 次印刷
印　　数	1—2050 套
书　　号	ISBN 978-7-5504-3776-0
定　　价	198.00 元（套）